BIOGRAPHIES FOR KIDS

All about Martin Luther King Jr. Words That Changed America

Children's Biographies of Famous People Books

Speedy Publishing LLC
40 E. Main St. #1156
Newark, DE 19711
www.speedypublishing.com

WHO WAS MARTIN LUTHER KING, JR.?

WHY IS HE FAMOUS?

WHAT DID HE DO TO BE FOREVER CARVED IN THE HEARTS OF THE PEOPLE?

Martin Luther King, Jr. was the second child of Martin Luther King, Sr. He was born on January 15, 1929 in Atlanta, Georgia.

OUT OF THE MOUNTAIN OF DESPAIR

He was a Baptist
minister and a civil
rights activist.
He played a very
important role in
American civil rights
from the mid-1950s
to 1968.

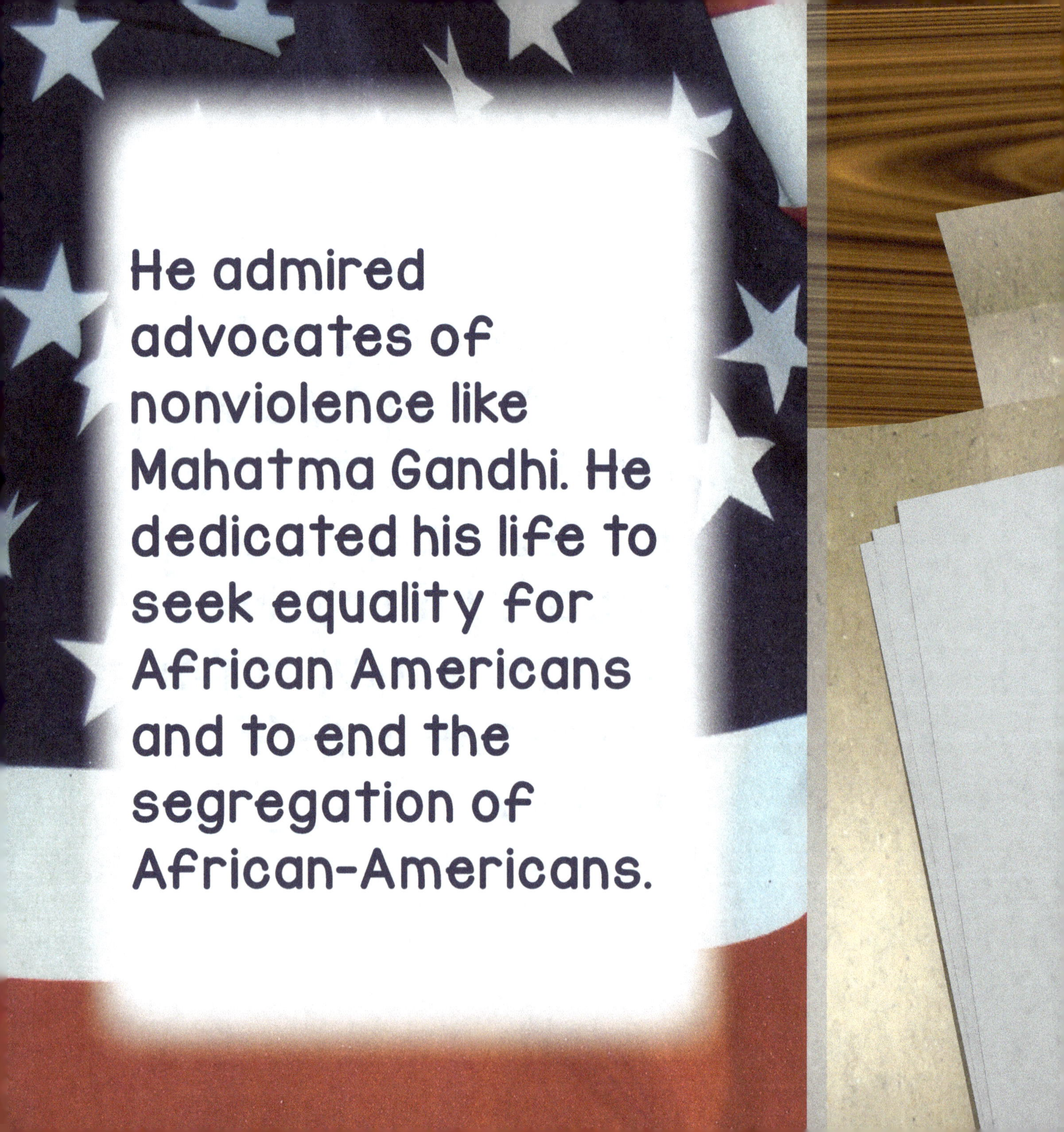
He admired
advocates of
nonviolence like
Mahatma Gandhi. He
dedicated his life to
seek equality for
African Americans
and to end the
segregation of
African-Americans.

RACE
DISCRIMINATION

His devoted action led to the creation of the Civil Rights Act of 1964 and the Voting Rights Act of 1965. In 1964, he received the Nobel Peace Prize Award.

In his early years, he attended segregated public schools and he studied medicine and law at Morehouse College.

King earned
his doctorate
in systematic
theology at Boston
University.

In 1953, he married Coretta Scott, a young singer who studied at the New England Conservatory of Music. They had four children.

For less than a year,
the King family lived in
Montgomery. He became the
protest's leader and official
spokesman.

He and other civil rights activists founded the Southern Christian Leadership Conference (SCLC).

HAVE A DREAM

He became the president of this group. The group aimed to achieve full equality for African Americans through nonviolent movements.

Martin Luther King Jr. gave lectures against violent protests as he traveled across the country.

Marti

Luther King Jr. DR
SW

He also met with religious leaders, political leaders and activists. King, Jr. wrote the "Letter from Birmingham Jail", which was a civil rights manifesto.

It was an eloquent defense of civil disobedience for white clergymen who criticized him.

Martin Luther King Jr., together with civil rights and religious groups, organized the March on Washington.

This was a march for Jobs and Freedom. This was a peaceful political rally to protest the injustices towards African Americans.

ALL VETERANS UNITE IN OUR DRIVE FOR THE BONUS
WE DEMAND THE BONUS for ALL Veterans

The historical Washington March was attended by some 200,000 to 300,000 people and was regarded as a factor in the passage of the Civil Rights Act of 1964.

It was considered as the most important moment in the history of the American civil rights movement.

He delivered a very eloquent and famous speech, known as "I Have a Dream". This was a call for peace and equality. King, Jr. stood on the steps of the Lincoln Memorial as he delivered his most spirited speech.

He called for equality and peace. In his speech, he emphasized that all men were created equal. He was named the Man of the Year by TIME Magazine. While he was standing on the balcony of a motel in Memphis, on April 4, 1968, Martin Luther King Jr. was

assassinated. In
1983, President
Ronald Reagan
signed a bill in honor
of Martin Luther
King, Jr.

The commemoration
of his death became
a U.S. Federal
holiday, which was
first celebrated on
the third Monday of
January in 1986.

HAPPY MARTIN LUTHER KING DAY
18 th JAN
MLK DAY
I have a dream...

King, Jr. was one of
the most admired
African-American
leaders in history.
He was a very
eloquent man.

He was brave. He was nonviolent. He really had a dream for his people.

KIDS, DO YOU LIKE HIM?

ARE YOU ALSO WILLING TO STAND UP FOR WHAT YOU THINK IS RIGHT?

Visit
BABY PROFESSOR
EDUCATION KIDS
www.BabyProfessorBooks.com
to download Free Baby Professor eBooks
and view our catalog of new and exciting
Children's Books